THOMAS CRANE PUBLIC LIBRARY

QUINCY MASS

CITY APPROPRIATION

Learning About the
Human Body Systems

# Learning About the Nervous System

by Martha V. Gold

**Enslow Publishers, Inc.**
40 Industrial Road
Box 398
Berkeley Heights, NJ 07922
USA

http://www.enslow.com

Dedicated to my husband,
Tom Barron, and my son, Ian Barron.

Original edition published as *The Nervous System* in 2004.

**Library of Congress Cataloging-in-Publication Data**

Gold, Martha V.
  Learning about the nervous system / Martha V. Gold.
      p. cm. — (Learning about the human body systems)
  Summary: "Discover more about how this system works and read amazing facts about the brain and nervous
system"— Provided by publisher.
  Includes bibliographical references and index.
  ISBN 978-0-7660-4160-8
  1. Nervous system—Juvenile literature.  I. Title.
  QP361.5.G65 2013
  612.8—dc23

                                                2012011103

Future editions:
Paperback ISBN:  978-1-4644-0241-8
ePUB ISBN:  978-1-4645-1157-8
PDF ISBN:  978-1-4646-1157-5

Printed in the United States of America

082012 Lake Book Manufacturing, Inc., Melrose Park, IL

10 9 8 7 6 5 4 3 2 1

**To Our Readers:** We have done our best to make sure all Internet addresses in this book were active and appropriate
when we went to press. However, the author and the publisher have no control over and assume no liability for the
material available on those Internet sites or on other Web sites they may link to. Any comments or suggestions can
be sent by e-mail to comments@enslow.com or to the address on the back cover.

♻ Enslow Publishers, Inc., is committed to printing our books on recycled paper. The paper in every book
contains 10% to 30% post-consumer waste (PCW). The cover board on the outside of each book contains 100%
PCW. Our goal is to do our part to help young people and the environment too!

**Photo Credits:** BananaStock/Thinkstock, p. 38 (nose); © Digital Stock, Corbis Corp., p. 9; Jupiterimages/
Photos.com, p. 1; © Life Art, Williams & Wilkins, pp. 4, 7, 12, 13, 16, 18, 23, 38 (brain); © Lisa Turay/
Photos.com, p. 34; Photodisc, p. 39; © Susan Dudley Gold, p. 21; The National Library of Medicine, p. 30.

**Cover Photo:** Shutterstock.com

# Contents

# NERVOUS SYSTEM

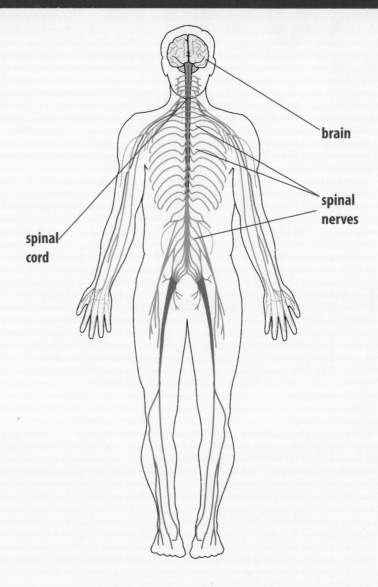

brain

spinal
nerves

spinal
cord

# What Is the Nervous System?

# Chapter 1

What do the following activities have in common?

- Running to catch a bus
- Breathing
- Figuring out how to put together a puzzle
- Jerking your hand away from a hot pan
- Swallowing food

Each is made possible by the nervous system, which controls the body's internal functions. The nervous system also directs our body's voluntary and involuntary actions. In fact, every task the body performs involves the nervous system. The endocrine system also controls certain body functions. The two systems work together.

The main parts of the nervous system are the **central nervous system** (CNS) and the **peripheral nervous system**.

## Central Nervous System

The central nervous system is the most complex collection of matter that exists. It consists of the brain and the spinal cord. The brain is a spongy mass of pinkish-gray tissue that looks like a large walnut. It is divided into two halves that lie on the left and the right sides of the head. The halves are called hemispheres. A thick band of nerve fibers called the **corpus callosum** connects the halves.

An adult brain weighs about 3 pounds (1,300 to 1,400 grams). A newborn baby's brain weighs slightly more than three-quarters of a pound (340 to 400 grams).[1] The brain grows rapidly in children. By the time a person turns twelve the brain has reached adult size.[2]

The skull covers the brain and protects it. Three layers of tissue called **meninges** lie between the brain and the skull and shield the brain from harm. The outer layer of the meninges is called the dura mater. This tough, thick layer keeps the brain in place. The inner layer, the pia mater, lies closest to the brain. The center layer is called the arachnoid.

Spaces in the brain called **ventricles** contain a clear liquid. This liquid, the **cerebrospinal fluid**, bathes the brain, surrounding it and protecting it from injury. The fluid keeps the brain afloat inside the skull. This takes the pressure off the base of the brain.

The brain serves as the central command center for the entire body. It controls every body function, from digesting food to throwing a ball to understanding language. The brain is divided into three basic parts: the **cerebrum**, the **brain stem** and related systems, and the **cerebellum**. The cerebrum is the largest part of the brain. The **cerebral cortex**, the outer layer of the

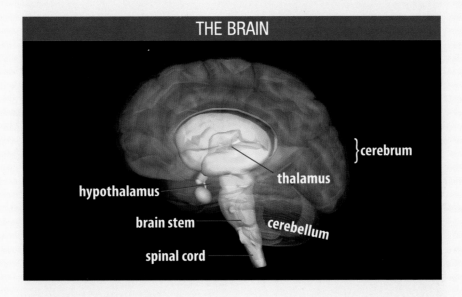

**THE BRAIN**

cerebrum

thalamus

hypothalamus

brain stem

cerebellum

spinal cord

cerebrum, carries out many of the brain's tasks such as thinking, understanding language, and reasoning. Billions of nerve cells, also called neurons, are crammed into this thin, wrinkled layer of the brain.[3] The **motor cortex**, a thin strip located in the cerebral cortex, is responsible for voluntary movement. When a person reaches for a glass of juice, the motor cortex commands the muscles in the arm and hand to close around the glass and lift it from the table.

Beneath the cerebrum lie several structures that control involuntary or automatic body functions. The **thalamus**, the section directly under the cerebrum, lies deep in the core of the brain. It looks like a barbell. It has two oval masses, one inside each half, that are joined by a bridge. The thalamus sorts out information from four of the senses: sight, hearing, taste, and touch. It sends signals related to these senses to the cerebral cortex. Messages relating to smell, unlike the other senses, bypass the thalamus and go directly to the cerebral cortex.[4]

The tiny **hypothalamus** occupies an area just below the thalamus at the base of the brain. Though only the size of a thumbnail, it has several big jobs. The hypothalamus acts like a central computer that sends orders to other computers. It works with the nervous system and the endocrine system to keep the body functioning smoothly.

The endocrine system, like the nervous system, relays instructions to parts of the body. It does this by releasing **hormones** that tell the body to do certain things, such as convert food into energy. Hormones are chemicals released by glands and carried by the blood.

The hypothalamus works with other parts of the nervous system to make the body react to strong emotions such as rage, fear, and pleasure. If a person has a nightmare or sees an angry dog, the hypothalamus tells the heart to beat faster and the lungs to take shallow, quick breaths. The hypothalamus also regulates body temperature and controls hunger and thirst.

The brain stem forms a stalk that runs from the center of the brain. It contains the **midbrain**, the **pons**, and the **medulla**. These brain parts control breathing, heart rate, blood pressure, pupil dilation, and the vomiting reflex, among other things. They work with the cerebellum to control muscle tone. This region also works with the motor cortex to control voluntary movement.

The **amygdala** and the **hippocampus** lie below the brain stem. These are part of the **limbic system**, a group of structures that control emotions. The two small, almond-shaped structures of the amygdala are made up of nerve cells. This part of the brain processes and responds to sensory information from the cerebral cortex. When a perfume reminds you of your mother, the amygdala is at work. Short-term memories are stored in the hippocampus. The cerebral cortex is believed to store long-term memory.

The cerebellum coordinates complex tasks such as learning to play a musical instrument, then stores the information.

In the back of the brain lies the cerebellum, often called the "little brain." With two halves each the size of a tennis ball, it looks like a small cerebral cortex. This is the second largest part of the human brain. It coordinates complex movements such as walking. The cerebellum then stores the information about the movement. When a person rides a bicycle or learns to play the piano, the motor cortex uses this stored information to tell the muscles involved to contract and relax as needed.

The second part of the central nervous system, the spinal cord, lies just below the brain stem. It is made up of nerve fibers. These fibers pass information from the rest of the body to the brain and from the brain to muscles and nerve cells. The spinal column or backbone—a series of hollow bones called vertebrae that are linked together—surround the spinal cord and protect it. Small disks of cartilage—like tiny pillows—separate the vertebrae. Ligaments, tough bands of tissue, hold the vertebrae in place.

## Peripheral Nervous System

The brain and the spinal cord work with the peripheral nervous system. This system forms a vast network of neurons. These neurons carry messages back and forth between the body and the spinal cord and the brain. The peripheral nerves also help direct all involuntary and voluntary movement. For instance, during a game of kickball the peripheral nerves send a message to a player's brain to tell the heart to beat faster.

The peripheral nervous system is divided into two parts, the **somatic nervous system** and the **autonomic nervous system**. The somatic nervous system controls most voluntary movement. When a person picks up a water glass, the somatic nervous system sends impulses from the cerebral cortex to the neurons in the arm and hand to grasp the glass.

The autonomic nervous system controls all involuntary or automatic movement. This includes breathing, heartbeat, and digestion. The autonomic nervous system consists of two parts that work in opposite ways on the body's organs. The sympathetic system calls the body into action when danger threatens. It makes the heart beat faster, causes the pupils to dilate, and slows digestion. When the danger has passed, the parasympathetic system tells the body to relax. It tells the heart to slow down and the stomach to begin digesting food. The parasympathetic system works during calm times such as after a meal or while watching TV.

# Members of the Team

Like a well-oiled machine, the body relies on its parts to operate. The nervous system, in turn, depends on its many parts to perform their duties. Each part has an important role to play.

## The Complex Brain

The brain is the most complex member of the nervous system. People look in awe at advancements in technology. But even the most sophisticated computer cannot equal the abilities of the human brain. Together with the rest of the nervous system, the brain keeps our bodies working. It figures out math problems, makes us cry during sad movies, and enables us to recognize our mother's perfume. While a computer can perform calculations much more quickly than a human, it cannot carry out as many tasks at once as the brain. Perhaps the most important difference between the two is consciousness. Humans know they are here. A computer is not conscious of its being or its presence on earth or anything else.

The human brain weighs only about three pounds. It consists primarily of gelatin-like tissue. In the outer layers is the brain's gray matter, where nerve cell bodies are located. This is where most of the information between cells is exchanged. The inner areas of the brain are made up of white matter. **Axons**—long, thin fibers that extend from neurons—are located in the white matter. Messages speed along these fibers.

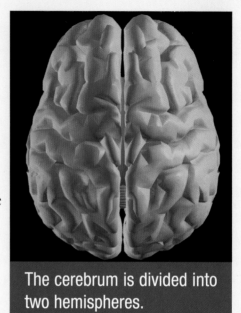

The cerebrum is divided into two hemispheres.

The cerebrum, the largest part of the brain, has two hemispheres. These halves are divided into four sections, or lobes: frontal lobes, parietal lobes, temporal lobes, and occipital lobes. Each has distinct and specific functions.

Frontal lobes lie behind the forehead. They regulate reasoning, planning, speech, movement, emotions, and problem solving. These lobes go into action when a person plans a trip, imagines the future, or argues a point. The frontal lobes act as short-term storage sites, allowing a person to remember one idea while considering other ideas. The back of the frontal lobes controls voluntary movement.

Behind the frontal lobes lie the parietal lobes. They receive information from the rest of the body about touch, pressure, temperature, and pain. These lobes tell a person to enjoy the

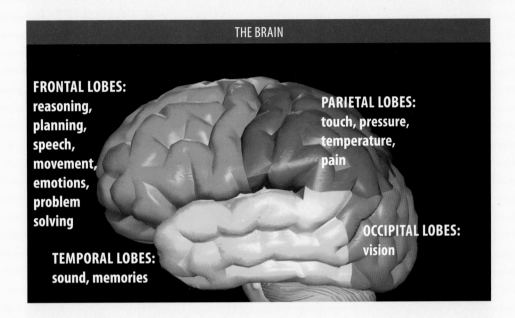

**THE BRAIN**

**FRONTAL LOBES:** reasoning, planning, speech, movement, emotions, problem solving

**PARIETAL LOBES:** touch, pressure, temperature, pain

**OCCIPITAL LOBES:** vision

**TEMPORAL LOBES:** sound, memories

taste, the aroma, and the texture of a good meal. They also signal pain when something strikes or injures the body. A person also uses the parietal lobes when reading or doing arithmetic.[1]

The temporal lobes lie below the parietal and frontal lobes. The top section recognizes sound. The hippocampus, at the bottom of the lobes, forms and retrieves memories. Other parts of these lobes connect memories to sensations of taste, sound, sight, and touch.

The occipital lobes in the back of the head allow us to see. These lobes process images from the eyes and link that information with images stored in memory. Damage to the occipital lobes can cause blindness.

Inside the lobes, certain areas control specific functions such as thinking, movement, and touch. Some span across more than one lobe. Some areas enable people to solve problems, have complex ideas, and feel emotion. Other areas coordinate movement and instruct the muscles to move. Still others process information collected from the eyes, ears, body, nose, and mouth.

Each hemisphere or side of the brain controls and senses the opposite side of the body. This means that the left side of the brain controls the muscles on the right side of the body, and the right side of the brain controls the muscles on the left side of the body. Each side also controls certain actions or behaviors.

The left hemisphere controls language, mathematics, and logic for most right-handed people. The right hemisphere enables people to recognize faces, judge distance, recall scenery, and appreciate music.[2] The parts of the brain that control language and speech are found in the left hemispheres of right-handed people and in the right hemispheres of left-handed people.

## Spinal Cord Highway

The spinal cord is like a superhighway that runs between the brain and the peripheral nervous system. The brain sends messages along the nerves in the spinal cord to tell different parts of the body to work. The peripheral nervous system also sends messages along the spinal cord to the brain from various parts of the body.

The spinal cord is about eighteen inches long in men and seventeen inches long in women. It begins in the neck and runs down the center of the back to below the waist. As in the brain, the meninges surrounds the spinal cord. Thirty-three vertebrae encircle the spinal cord and protect it.

Like the brain, the spinal cord has gray and white matter. In the spinal cord, however, the gray matter is surrounded by white matter. The top part of the spinal cord is also packed with white matter. This is because there are many axons going up to the brain from the spinal cord and down to different segments of the spinal cord. In the lower segments of the spinal cord, there is less white matter because there are fewer axons traveling to and from the brain from that area.

## Cranial and Spinal Nerves

Nerves outside the brain and the spinal cord—the peripheral nervous system—serve as the body's messengers. They bring information from the sense organs and muscles to the brain and from the brain to muscles, glands, and internal organs.

Twelve pairs of **cranial nerves** extend from the brain's center stalk. Most of these nerves connect to various parts of the brain stem. These nerves are known by their names and also by their numbers. They control eye movement, facial expression, hearing, and balance. They also control the muscles for chewing and cause the mouth to water. The vagus nerve, the longest of the cranial nerves, reaches into the abdomen. It controls the larynx muscles, heart rate, and impulses that trigger digestion.

Thirty-one pairs of spinal nerves lead from the spinal cord, through the openings between the vertebrae, and into the chest, abdomen, arms, and legs. Like cranial nerves, they carry information both to and from the brain.

## Neurons

Neurons, the cells of the nervous system, come in many different shapes and sizes. The smallest have cell bodies that are only 4 microns wide. The biggest neurons have cell bodies

that are 100 microns wide.
One micron is equal to one
thousandth of a millimeter
and is too small to be seen
with the naked eye.[3]

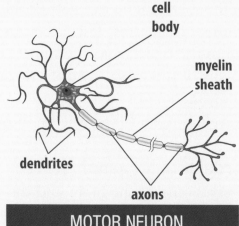

**MOTOR NEURON**

Neurons grow nerve
fibers that extend through-
out the body. These fibers
are called **dendrites** and
axons. Dendrites look like
tree branches. They receive
nerve impulses and send them to the cell body. The impulses
then pass to the axon at the other side of the cell. Axons
extend outward from the neuron in a thin line. Layers of cells
wrap around the axons to protect them. These insulated layers
are called the **myelin sheath**. The shortest axons are less than
an inch and the longest ones are more than three feet long.
The end of the axon branches off into sac-like structures.
These structures send messages to other neurons.

Sensory neurons carry impulses to the spinal cord
and the brain. They provide the brain with information
collected by the senses about the environment and the
body. Motor neurons carry instructions from the brain to
the muscles and glands. Interneurons serve as the central
office, routing incoming and outgoing messages to the
proper paths.

## Sensory Organs

The five senses—sight, smell, hearing, taste, and touch—provide important information that helps us function in the world. Each sense gives us a different view of life around us. The nervous system carries each interesting report from the senses to the brain. The brain, in turn, interprets the signals and responds to them. As a result, our mouth waters at the smell of a Thanksgiving turkey roasting in the oven. The spicy tang of chili can warm our whole body. And the sound of a favorite rap tune can start our foot tapping.

Each sensory organ has special tools to help interpret the world around us. Two eyes located in the front of the face allow people to judge distance. The eye contains specialized cells called rods and cones because of their shape. Cones allow us to see colors. Rods help us locate things in dim light. These cells are in the retina, a multilayer of tissue that lines the inner eyeball.

Cells in the skin called sensory receptors register touch, pressure, pain, and temperature. If someone touches a person's arm, one set of receptors tells that person's brain whether the hand is cold or warm. Another set of receptors tells how much pressure is exerted. If the arm is shaken, other receptors report the amount of vibration. If someone squeezes the arm, the receptors issue a pain report. This information travels up a network of nerve cells to the brain.

Likewise, the nose uses its own equipment to identify smells. When the aroma of freshly baked bread wafts through the air, the nostrils pick up the scent molecules. After being dissolved, the molecules travel up the nasal passage, where receptor cells absorb them. These cells translate the odors into signals, which are sent to the brain. Most people can smell up to ten thousand different odors.[4]

Sounds travel through the air in the form of waves. The outer ear captures the sound waves, which then travel through the auditory canal to the eardrum, causing it to vibrate. The eardrum's vibrations move the ham-

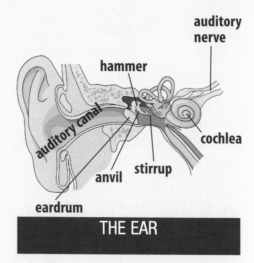

auditory nerve

hammer

auditory canal

cochlea

stirrup

anvil

eardrum

**THE EAR**

mer (malleus), a tiny bone in the middle ear that is connected to the eardrum, from side to side. This causes a chain reaction, moving the anvil (incus), which is attached to the hammer, and then the stirrup (stapes), which is next to the anvil. The movement causes the stirrup to push against the fluid in the adjoining cochlea in the inner ear. This creates waves in the fluid. Thin fibers stretch across the cochlea. As the waves pass through, the fibers vibrate.

High-pitched sounds cause vibrations of the shorter fibers, while lower-pitched sounds cause the longer fibers to vibrate. Tiny hair cells in the cochlea pick up the vibrations and send electrical impulses to the auditory nerve, which carries the message to the brain. There, the cerebral cortex interprets the message, and we hear the sounds that began the whole process!

There are about ten thousand taste buds on the human tongue. Taste buds tell people whether something is sweet, sour, salty, or bitter. Three cranial nerves in the tongue send taste information to the brain.

# How Does the Nervous System Work?

The body's message system operates like a complex telephone switchboard. Messages speed along a network of neurons in the same way a telephone call travels through telephone lines. Instead of telephone numbers, chemicals direct the message to its correct destination. These chemicals are called **neurotransmitters**.

The neurons transmit signals from one cell to another. The message travels through each neuron to the axon that extends from the cell. When the message reaches the end of the axon, neurotransmitters carry the signal across the gap to the receptors of the next nerve cell. The gap is called a **synapse** or synaptic gap.

Neurotransmitters make sure messages go to the right places. They are like keys; the receptors serve as locks. The neurotransmitter unlocks the receptor and sends the message across the synapse and on its way to the next neuron.[1]

| SOME COMMON NEUROTRANSMITTERS | |
|---|---|
| Acetylcholine | slows heart muscle; stimulates other muscles |
| Dopamine | controls movement; affects emotions, feelings of pleasure, pain |
| Epinephrine | speeds heart rate; stimulates body's use of glucose |
| GABA (gamma-aminobutyric acid) | induces relaxation, sleep; controls muscle contractions |
| Norepinephrine | affects dreams, moods, alertness |
| Serotonin | regulates body temperature, eating, sleep, sensation of pain and other senses |

There are more than twenty-four known neurotransmitters. That list is expected to grow as scientists study other substances believed to be neurotransmitters. Acetylcholine, for example, has two jobs. It tells skeletal muscles to go to work, and it also slows down the heart muscle. The neurotransmitter serotonin slows down reactions. It regulates pain, sensory perception, eating, sleep, and body temperature.

Other neurotransmitters—epinephrine, dopamine, and norepinephrine—affect the body in different ways. Epinephrine, or adrenaline, is released into the bloodstream at times of acute danger or stress. For example, when an angry bully threatens someone, that person's epinephrine speeds up the heart rate and causes the person to breathe faster. That enables the person to run away or to stand up to the bully. (This is called the "flight or fight" syndrome.) Dopamine plays a big role in emotional, mental, and motor functions. It sometimes acts as an "off" switch, shutting off the release of certain chemicals. It also helps to control movement. Norepinephrine is closely related to epinephrine. It sometimes blocks the action of other neurotransmitters. It can make a person alert but is also linked to sleep and moods.

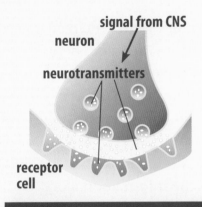

signal from CNS

neuron

neurotransmitters

receptor cell

SYNAPSE

**Peptides** are chains of amino acids (organic compounds needed to sustain life). Most are not real neurotransmitters, but they adjust or fine-tune the neurotransmitters' effects. Neurotransmitters act quickly. Peptides bring about much more gradual changes. They have been linked to easing pain, learning, moods, and a decrease in appetite. There are many different peptides that regulate a wide variety of body functions. Some of the better known peptides include endorphins, which reduce the feelings of pain; insulin, which controls blood sugar levels; and prolactin, which stimulates the production of milk in pregnant women.

## How Nerves Communicate

While walking one evening, a girl looks down to see that she is about to step on a skunk. Immediately her heart starts beating faster and her knees feel weak. Her first thought is to run. Then she remembers that sudden movements startle animals. Not wanting to upset the skunk, she backs up slowly before turning to run.

During that incident the girl's brain and nervous system sent many messages between the body and the brain. The messages traveled along a network of neurons to the brain and from the brain to other parts of the body.

The brain keeps tight control of this message delivery system to avoid "wrong numbers." A single receiving neuron can have thousands of receptor sites. Each neuron decides whether to pass the information along.

When communication between cells gets out of balance, a person may develop serious conditions such as epilepsy and memory loss.[2]

Once the message reaches its final destination, it tells the muscle or organ to act. At first the girl wanted to run when she saw the skunk. That was because the cerebral cortex identified the skunk as dangerous. The sympathetic nervous system sent a message to the heart to beat faster, to the sweat glands to begin working, and to the hair follicles to make hair stand up.

At the same time the cerebellum sent messages to the leg muscles to stop walking and to prepare to run away. The messages traveled from the cerebellum to the spinal cord and to the thigh and calf muscles. The messages ordered the muscles to contract to make the legs move.

## Higher Order Thinking

Before running, the girl remembered that sudden movements startle animals. She knew skunks spray a horrible, stinky liquid when startled. She decided not to run but to back away slowly to avoid scaring the skunk. By using the facts

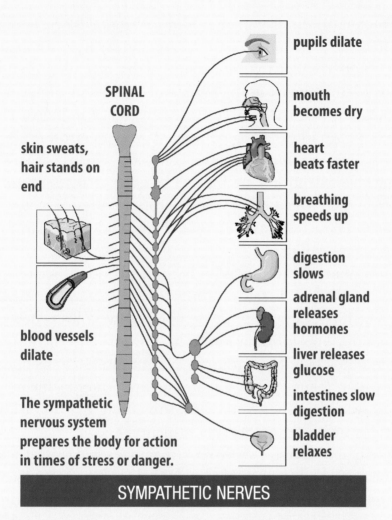

SPINAL
CORD

pupils dilate

mouth
becomes dry

heart
beats faster

breathing
speeds up

digestion
slows

adrenal gland
releases
hormones

liver releases
glucose

intestines slow
digestion

bladder
relaxes

skin sweats,
hair stands on
end

blood vessels
dilate

The sympathetic
nervous system
prepares the body for action
in times of stress or danger.

## SYMPATHETIC NERVES

to analyze the situation, the girl engaged in higher order thinking. Higher order thinking involves reasoning, analysis, imagination, and creativity.

What happens in the brain when a person thinks, reasons, creates, or forms memories? Scientists can identify the parts of the brain used in thinking. But how thinking actually takes place remains one of the biggest mysteries in neuroscience.

Thinking and reasoning occur in the frontal lobes. Studies show that the prefrontal cortex, located in the frontal lobes, becomes active when a person thinks. What scientists do not know is what happens in the brain when a person thinks. One theory is that the brain generates waves of impulses. These impulses move along neurons. When a person thinks of a new idea, the impulses travel across the synapse to new neurons. New dendrites are formed or other changes occur that strengthen the link between neurons and result in new responses. These responses become the new ideas or learning that humans acquire.[3]

How does new information become memory? Scientists believe that chemicals carry information to memory storage areas. The hippocampus in the temporal lobe collects new information. This information forms a short-term memory. The brain holds short-term memories for just a few seconds. A short-term memory will stay in the hippocampus for no more than 20 seconds. When you repeat something that someone else just said, you are using short-term memory.

The brain processes short-term memories and shifts them into the frontal lobe. There they are stored as long-term memories. Long-term memories can stay in our brains for an hour, a day, or many years. When you memorize your phone number or a poem, you rely on long-term memory. Recent studies show that the neurotransmitter dopamine may help carry knowledge to the frontal lobes. It also may play a role in thinking and reasoning.[4]

Researchers believe that memory is stored when certain factors are in place during a synapse. These factors change the structures of certain cells. In the process of changing the structure of the cells, memories are formed. One study of rats revealed that certain neurons released the neurotransmitter glutamate during the synapse process. This in turn caused structural changes in the cells. These changes made an imprint on the brain, which created memories.[5]

Scientists have learned many things about the way the brain works, but much remains unknown. Research into artificial intelligence may solve some of the mysteries. Artificial intelligence is the process of making a computer that can think like a human being.

## Reticular Network

Have you ever wondered how a person can concentrate on a book in a busy, noisy room? How a mother can sleep through a loud thunderstorm but wake up when her baby stirs in the next room?

Millions of messages pass through the brain every second. Most of the messages from the senses travel through the thalamus into the cerebral cortex. Messages directing motor activities are also routed through the thalamus. A remarkable system of neurons and fibers called the **reticular formation** sorts through this maze of messages. Located inside the brain stem, it acts like a filter for the many things that act on the nervous system. Only the size of the little finger, the reticular formation keeps us awake and alert and allows us to react to certain impulses and ignore others. It also plays a role in movement and transmitting sensations of pain, temperature, and touch.[6]

# Chapter 4

# Disorders and Disease

A human brain has more than 100 billion neurons—so many that a person counting one neuron per second would take more than three thousand years to count them all.

As people age, brain cells die and are not replaced. Eventually, after many, many years, the brain shrinks, protein levels decrease, and sometimes the level of neurotransmitters drops. The grooves in the brain, called sulci, widen. This often leads to memory problems in elderly people.

## Neurological Disorders

For most, memory problems are not serious and people simply become a little more forgetful as they age. However, dementia, a deterioration of the brain, is a problem for 5 to 10 percent of people who are sixty-five and older. Alzheimer's disease is a common form of dementia. People with Alzheimer's gradually lose their memory. As the disease becomes worse, the person needs help bathing, eating, and going to the bathroom. There is no cure yet. Scientists have been unable to determine the exact cause of Alzheimer's. When examined after death, the brains of some Alzheimer's patients show tangled neuron fibers and patches of protein called plaques. Scientists believe these interfere with the ability of neurons to send messages.

Elderly people are more likely to get neurological diseases (those affecting the nervous system), though most of these disorders can affect people of any age. These diseases change the way the body functions.

Parkinson's disease occurs when certain cells in the midbrain are lost. This area produces dopamine, which enables people to move in smooth, steady motions. People with Parkinson's disease shake uncontrollably, have stiff muscles, and must move slowly. There is no cure, but medicines and therapy can help a person with the disease. Parkinson's occurs most often in elderly people, but it can also afflict younger people.

Some neurological disorders are congenital, meaning that a person is born with the disorder. One of the most common of these disorders is spina bifida. In spina bifida the vertebrae and the muscles do not surround the spinal cord. Pregnant women take folic acid to help prevent these disorders in their babies. Doctors believe that environmental and genetic factors may play a role in some congenital diseases.

Learning disabilities, also neurological disorders, make it hard for people to learn certain skills. People with dyslexia, for example, have problems processing words. They may mix up the order of words or see letters in reverse. This makes it difficult to learn how to read.

The electronic processes in the brain are disrupted in people who have epilepsy. Neurons in the cerebral hemispheres misfire and create abnormal electrical activity. People with epilepsy have repeated seizures. A seizure causes a person to lose control of his body. About half of epilepsy cases are caused by damage to the brain.

## Brain Damage and Spinal Cord Injuries

Although the brain and spinal cord are well cushioned, they can still be injured. An estimated 1.7 million people in the United States suffer a traumatic brain injury each year. [1] Nearly twelve thousand Americans seriously injure their spinal cords every year.

Injuries to the head range from a mild concussion to severe trauma that causes internal bleeding. A concussion is a mild injury or bruise to the brain. It can cause headaches, loss of consciousness, nausea, and memory problems.

Serious head injuries can cause bleeding or pressure in the brain. The blood itself can damage the brain, or it can cause nearby tissue to swell, increasing pressure on the brain. As a result, a person can become agitated, confused, or sluggish. Problems with speech, vision, or muscle weakness may occur. In the most serious cases, swelling or bleeding will cause coma or death. A person in a coma usually seems to be asleep. Coma usually lasts only a few days or weeks. But sometimes a person never wakes up and eventually dies.

Injuries to the spinal cord are always serious. They can result in paralysis or death. More than half of all spinal cord injuries happen to people between the ages of sixteen and thirty. Men are four times more likely to have spinal cord injuries than women.[2] Motor vehicle accidents lead to more spinal injuries than any other cause. Acts of violence, falls, and sports also cause many injuries of this type.

## Toxic Chemicals

Exposure to toxic chemicals can damage the brain. Lead damages the myelin and axons of peripheral nerves. Old paint is a major source of lead. In children, lead exposure has been linked to lower intelligence, learning disabilities, slow growth, behavior problems, and hearing loss. Adults poisoned by lead may have muscle and joint pain, memory problems, and other symptoms.

Methyl mercury, another harmful substance, is found in old thermometers, among other places. It targets and kills neurons in certain areas of the nervous system, including the cerebellum. Mercury is especially dangerous to the developing fetus.[3]

## Mental Illnesses

Mental illness affects moods, the ability to reason, and emotions. People once thought mental illness was caused by evil spirits. Today many scientists believe that mental illness occurs when chemicals in the brain are out of balance. Bipolar disorder and schizophrenia are two examples of mental illness. People with bipolar disorder swing between periods of deep depression and extreme joy or high energy. Studies have found lesions in the white matter of the brains of several people who have bipolar disorder. Other research of people with the disorder has revealed unusual activity in different parts of the brain, including the prefrontal cortex.[4]

29

People with schizophrenia cannot tell the difference between what is real and what is imagined. They may have hallucinations that cause them to think that they hear, see, smell, or feel things that don't exist. Scientists have discovered that many people with schizophrenia have larger than normal ventricles and other brain abnormalities.[5]

An 1848 case showed the link between the brain and a person's personality. A man named Phineas Gage was working on a railroad in Vermont when a three-and-a-half-foot spike went through his head. He survived, but his personality changed dramatically. A serious young man known as a good worker before the accident, he began swearing and became stubborn and unreliable after his brain injury. Researchers surmised that the front part of Gage's brain damaged by the spike controlled parts of his personality.[6]

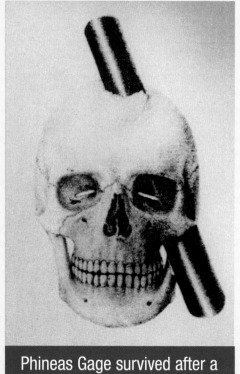

Phineas Gage survived after a spike went through his head.

## Headaches and Tumors

The brain cannot feel pain. But some of the cranial nerves, the muscles of the head, and blood vessels along the surface and at the base of the brain can hurt. Stress, tense muscles, and dilated blood vessels can make these areas painful. Certain foods, odors, menstrual periods, and changes in weather can also trigger headaches.

Tumors can also cause headaches and other problems. A brain tumor pushes healthy cells out of the way, squeezing them against the skull. This causes pressure in the brain, which keeps it from working properly. A brain tumor can cause paralysis, behavior changes, and dizziness. A tumor can be cancerous (malignant) or not cancerous (benign). While benign tumors are less dangerous, they can still harm the brain. Though brain tumors are very rare.

## Drugs and the Brain

Drugs abused over a long period of time damage the brain. For example, cocaine, a stimulant, can increase blood pressure and cause bleeding in the brain or a stroke. Heavy alcohol use can damage the frontal lobes and prevent the body from absorbing vitamin B-1. This can cause memory loss, confusion, and lack of coordination.[7]

Diseases caused by smoking cigarettes kills more than 400,000 Americans each year.[8] Nicotine, a substance in tobacco, takes on the role of a neurotransmitter in the nervous system. As a result, the body makes less of the natural neurotransmitter. When a person tries to stop smoking, he or she craves nicotine. This is because there is much less of the neurotransmitter than the body is used to. This response is called addiction, which means the body craves a certain substance even though it is unhealthy. The same process occurs when people become addicted to drugs.

# Staying Healthy

The brain can be compared to a car. A car needs certain things to run: gas, oil, brake fluid, transmission fluid, and antifreeze. Likewise, the brain needs certain nutrients to work: glucose, protein, vitamins, minerals, and fats. Each plays a special role in keeping the brain healthy.

## Eating for Good Health

Because the nervous system is responsible for so many bodily functions, it is important to keep it healthy. Eating well and avoiding drugs, alcohol, and other harmful substances help keep the brain in top physical condition.

Glucose provides the fuel for the brain. Eating carbohydrates—compounds found in grains, certain vegetables, and fruit—keeps the brain supplied with the glucose it needs. Protein and fat help keep brain tissue healthy and the brain running smoothly. Protein and fat also contribute to healthy myelin, the fatty layers that protect axons. Proteins are large molecules made from long chains of amino acids.

Certain fats are found in vegetable oils and fish oils such as cod liver oil. People who do not get enough fat may have problems with vision. Animal studies show that diets low in certain fats interfere with learning, reduce motivation, and cause problems with motor activities. Too little fat in the diet may hurt frontal lobe systems that use the neurotransmitters dopamine and serotonin.[1] Other fats may affect the release of neurotransmitters and the brain's ability to use glucose.

The brain of a fetus goes through rapid growth between the tenth and the eighteenth week of pregnancy and during a child's first two years of life. A poor diet can slow the growth of the nervous system or damage it. Babies whose mothers did not get enough to eat during pregnancy may be mentally retarded or have behavioral problems. Starvation, bad diet, damage to the digestive system, infection, and alcoholism can all result in a lack of vitamins and minerals that is harmful to the brain.

## Preventing Injuries

Car, plane, and truck accidents are a leading cause of brain injuries. Almost 300,000 brain injuries occur each year due to motor vehicle accidents.[2] Seat belts and airbags help protect the head and the brain from injury during a crash. These safety features can also prevent spinal cord injuries. Wearing a helmet can reduce the risk to motorcyclists.

Sports injuries can damage the brain and the spinal cord. Bicyclists, skateboarders, and participants in other sports can greatly reduce the risk of injury by wearing a helmet. In one study, 47 percent of children hospitalized for bicycle-related injuries suffered brain injury. Experts say wearing helmets reduces the risk of brain injury by up to 88 percent.[3]

Soccer is another sport that is hard on the brain. Injuries occur when a player's head hits a goal post, another player, the ground, or the ball. Football players wear helmets; most soccer players do not. Learning how to head-butt the ball properly, using smaller balls and padded goalposts, and not allowing young players to hit the ball with their head can make this game safer.

Many brain injuries could be avoided if people wore helmets while riding bikes or playing sports.

When playing sports, people should always use a helmet and other safety equipment. Avoid hitting goal posts and diving headfirst. Use spotters—who can catch participants if they fall—in gymnastics and ice skating.

Gunshots, fights, and other acts of violence result in many injuries to the spinal cord and brain. Avoiding violent situations and keeping guns away from children help reduce injuries. Falls can be prevented by using a stepladder to reach high places. Safety gates on windows and stairs also help protect the brain and spinal cord from harm.

Mothers who are pregnant can reduce the chances of brain disorders in their children by not drinking alcohol or using illicit drugs. Avoiding such drugs and not drinking to excess can help prevent brain damage in adults as well.

Just as the body benefits from physical exercise, the brain improves with mental exercise. Tackling hard math problems and reading new books are ways to stretch the brain's ability. Painting, playing music, and writing can strengthen the brain as well. Studies have shown that idle brains lose more brain cells than those that keep active.

## Treatments

In many cases, there are no cures for diseases of the nervous system. But often doctors can treat such diseases with medications, surgery, or other methods. Most people who have epilepsy can control seizures with medication. When medication does not work, doctors may remove the part of the brain where the seizures start. In rare cases of severe epilepsy in children, doctors will remove one of the cerebral hemispheres. This can cause some motor problems, but children can learn to function after surgery.

Many mental illnesses can be treated with medication. Often a person can find help by talking about problems with an expert and learning ways to cope. In severe cases of depression, electric shock treatment may help. This slight electric current seems to restore the chemical balance in some people. However, people may not be able to remember parts of their past after the treatment ends.

Scientists are now working with several therapies to cure brain tumors. One treatment kills the tumor cells but leaves normal cells unharmed. Other treatments limit the spread of cancer or block the tumor's life-sustaining molecules.

Various forms of therapy can help people with spinal cord and brain injuries. Some people may never recover completely.

For many years scientists believed that the brain did not create new cells except in the olfactory bulb. For most of the brain this is true. When brain cells die, they are not replaced. This is why brains shrink in old age. Recently, however, scientists discovered that other parts of the brain can grow new cells. The hippocampus in the temporal lobe and parts of the frontal lobe can create new cells under certain conditions. This may occur when hormones in the hippocampus change or when the hippocampus is injured.[4] Scientists are now trying to understand why and how this occurs. This knowledge could help doctors grow new cells in brains that have been damaged. Such advances may someday help people with brain injuries.

The intricate and complex workings of the nervous system continue to fascinate scientists. While research has revealed amazing facts about the nervous system, much remains a mystery. With the help of technology, scientists continue to make new discoveries about the brain and the nervous system and how they work.

# Amazing but True

There is a popular belief that people use only 10 percent of their brains. That is not true. We use all of the brain. Damage to almost any part of the brain can have serious effects on behavior. That is one reason why neurosurgeons carefully map the brain before removing tissue during operations for epilepsy or brain tumors.[1]

Some people can function fairly well with only half a brain. In rare cases, children with epilepsy may have one cerebral hemisphere removed. They can do well after this surgery.[2]

A human brain accounts for only about 2 percent of the body's weight, but it uses 20 percent of the oxygen that enters the body.[3]

There are 1 billion neurons in a human spinal cord.[4]

A developing baby's neurons grow rapidly, at the rate of 250,000 every minute.[5]

The lightest known human brain, according to the Guinness Book of Records, belonged to a forty-six-year-old man. It weighed 1 pound, 8 ounces. The heaviest brain known belonged to a thirty-year-old man and weighed 5 pounds, 1.1 ounces.[6]

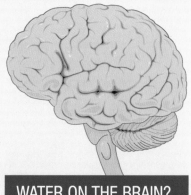

**WATER ON THE BRAIN?** More than 75 percent of the brain is water.

The cerebral cortex when laid out flat is the size of an unfolded newspaper, about two and one-half feet square.[7]

The brain of a gray whale weighs 4,317 grams, which is three times heavier than that of an average adult human.[8]

Most people think the sciatic nerve, which runs from the middle of the buttocks to mid-thigh, is the longest nerve in the body. The median and ulnar nerves are actually the longest

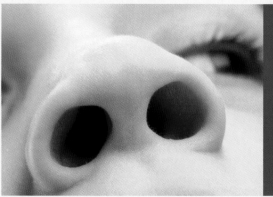

**WHAT'S THAT SMELL?** People can distinguish between three thousand and ten thousand different odors, some good and some bad. About 2 million people in the United States have no sense of smell.[9]

nerves in the body. They run from the shoulder to the wrist and are up to two feet long, depending on the length of the person's arm.[10]

At least 7 percent of males are color-blind and fewer than half of one percent of females are color-blind. Total color-blindness is very rare.[11]

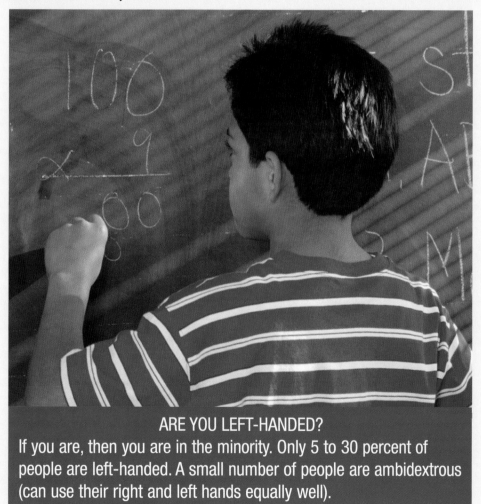

**ARE YOU LEFT-HANDED?**
If you are, then you are in the minority. Only 5 to 30 percent of people are left-handed. A small number of people are ambidextrous (can use their right and left hands equally well).

# Chapter Notes

## Chapter One: What Is the Nervous System?

1. Eric H. Chudler, "Brain Facts and Figures," n.d., <http://faculty. washington.edu/chudler/facts.html> (January 20, 2012).
2. Susan Greenfield, *The Human Brain* (New York: Basic Books, 1997), p. 101.
3. Chudler.
4. Sandra Ackerman, *Discovering the Brain* (Washington, D.C.: National Academy Press, 1992), p. 16.

## Chapter Two: Members of the Team

1. "Brain Basics: Know Your Brain," National Institute of Neurological Disorders and Stroke, n.d., <http://www.ninds. nih.gov/disorders/brain_basics/know_your_brain.htm> (January 20, 2012).
2. Sandra Ackerman, *Discovering the Brain* (Washington, D.C.: National Academy Press, 1992), p. 28.
3. Eric H. Chudler, "Brain Facts and Figures," n.d., <http://faculty. washington.edu/chudler/facts.html> (January 20, 2012).
4. William J. Cromie, "Researchers Sniff Out Secrets of Smell," Harvard University *Gazette*, April 8, 1999.

## Chapter Three: How Does the Nervous System Work?

1. Society for Neuroscience, *Brain Facts: A Primer on the Brain and the Nervous System*, Fourth Edition (Washington, D.C.: The Society for Neuroscience, 2002), pp. 4–5.
2. Sandra Ackerman, *Discovering the Brain* (Washington, D.C.: National Academy Press, 1992), p. 133.
3. Ibid., p. 135.
4. Ibid.
5. Ibid., pp. 139–140.
6. Judith Groch, *You and Your Brain* (New York: Harper & Row, 1963), p. 89.

## Chapter Four: Disorders and Disease

1. "Traumatic Brain Injury," Centers for Disease Control and Prevention, n.d., <http://www.cdc.gov/TraumaticBrainInjury/index.html> (January 23, 2012).
2. "Spinal Cord Injury Facts and Figures at a Glance," National Spinal Cord Injury Statistical Center, 2011, <https://www.nscisc.uab.edu/public_content/pdf/Facts%202011%20Feb%20Final.pdf> (Janaury 23, 2012).
3. "Mercury Study Report to Congress," U.S. Environmental Protection Agency, 1997, <http://www.epa.gov/mercury/report.htm> (January 24, 2012).
4. "Bipolar Disorder Research," National Institute of Mental Health, Fact Sheet #00-4502, April 2000.
5. Society for Neuroscience, *Brain Facts: A Primer on the Brain and the Nervous System*, Fourth Edition (Washington, D.C.: The Society for Neuroscience, 2002), p. 39.

6. "The Infinite Mind: Traumatic Brain Injury," National Public Radio, week of August 22, 2001.

7. "Thiamin Addition to Alcohol," Report 3 of the Council on Scientific Affairs, American Medical Association, Dec. 1996.

8. "Smoking and Tobacco Use: Fast Facts," Centers for Disease Control and Prevention, n.d., <http://www.cdc.gov/tobacco/ data_statistics/fact_sheets/fast_facts> (January 24, 2012).

## Chapter Five: Staying Healthy

1. Patricia Wolfe et al., "The Science of Nutrition," *Educational Leadership*, Vol. 57, No. 6, March 2000, p. 54–9.

2. "Traumatic Brain Injury in the United States: Emergency Department Visits, Hospitalizations and Deaths 2002–2006," National Center for Injury Prevention and Control, 2010, <http://www.cdc.gov/traumaticbraininjury/pdf/tbi_blue_book_ externalcause.pdf> (January 24, 2012).

3. "Bicycling and Skating Safety Fact Sheet," Safe Kids USA, n.d., <http://www.safekids.org/assets/docs/ourwork/research/ 2011-bicycle.pdf> (January 24, 2012).

4. Marguerite Holloway, "Young Cells in Old Brains," *Scientific American*, Vol. 285, No. 3, September 2001, pp. 30–31.

## Chapter Six: Amazing but True

1. "Myths About the Brain: Ten Percent and Counting," brainconnection.com, <http://www.brainconnection.com> (Dec. 22, 2002).

2. "Surgery for Epilepsy," National Institutes of Health, Consensus Statement, 8(2):1–20, Mar. 19–21, 1990.

3. Eric H. Chudler, "Brain Facts and Figures," <http://faculty. washington.edu/chudler/facts.html> (January 20, 2012).

4. Ibid.

5. Ibid.

6. Antonia Cunningham, Mark C. Young, eds., *Guinness Book of Records 2002* (New York: Bantam Books, 2002), pp. 7–8.

7. John Nolte, *The Human Brain: An Introduction to its Functional Anatomy*, Fifth Edition, (St. Louis, Mo.: Mosby, Inc., 2002), p. 525.

8. Chudler.

9. "Smell Disorders," National Institute on Deafness and Other Communication Disorders, n.d., <http://www.nidcd.nih.gov/ health/smelltaste/pages/smell.aspx> (January 20, 2012).

10. Washington University Medical School, *Mad Sci Network*, <http://www.madsci.org/circumnav/circumnav.html> (Aug. 7, 2002).

11. Geoffrey Montgomery, "Color Blindness: More Prevalent Among Males," A Report from the Howard Hughes Medical Institute, n.d., <http://www.hhmi.org/senses/b130.html> (January 24, 2012).

# Glossary

**amygdala**—Two almond-shaped brain structures that process and respond to nonverbal sensory information.

**autonomic nervous system**—Body system that controls all involuntary or automatic movement.

**axon**—Thin fiber that extends from a neuron and carries information from the cell.

**brain stem**—Area of the brain between the thalamus and spinal cord that contains the midbrain, the pons, and the medulla; responsible for the most basic functions of life such as breathing, heart rate, and blood pressure.

**central nervous system**—The brain and the spinal cord.

**cerebellum**—Part of the brain that processes data about movement, balance, and posture; behind the brain stem.

**cerebral cortex**—Thin, wrinkled layer that covers the cerebrum. Speech and reasoning are centered here.

**cerebrospinal fluid**—Clear fluid in the ventricular system.

**cerebrum**—Largest part of the brain, made up of two hemispheres. Directs higher order thinking such as language.

**corpus callosum**—Thick band of axons that connects the left and right hemispheres of the brain.

**cranial nerves**—Twelve pairs of nerves that carry messages between the brain and the senses, muscles, and organs.

**dendrite**—Branchlike extensions from the neuron cell body that take information to the cell body.

**hippocampus**—A structure at the base of the temporal lobe of the brain where short-term memory is kept.

**hormones**—Chemicals used by the body to send messages.

**hypothalamus**—Tiny structure at the base of the brain; helps controls body temperature, emotions, hunger, thirst.

**limbic system**—A group of structures that help control the emotional response to a given situation.

**medulla**—Part of the brain stem linked to breathing, respiration, and other involuntary activities.

**meninges**—A series of three membranes that cover the brain and the spinal cord.

**midbrain**—Part of the brainstem that controls eyeball movement and reflexes in the upper part of the body.

**motor cortex**—A thin strip located in the cerebral cortex that directs voluntary movement.

**myelin sheath**—Fatty substance that surrounds and insulates axons, speeding delivery of messages between neurons.

**neurotransmitters**—Chemicals that transmit information across the gap between one neuron and the next.

**peptides**—Chains of amino acids that can act as neurotransmitters or affect the way neurotransmitters respond.

**peripheral nervous system**—Network of neurons that runs between the brain and spinal cord and the rest of the body.

**pons**—Part of the brain stem that relays sensory and movement impulses.

**reticular formation**—Set of nerves and nerve fibers inside the brain stem that keeps the body alert.

**somatic nervous system**—Body system that controls voluntary movement.

**synapse**—Connection between the end of one neuron and that of another.

**thalamus**—Brain structure that receives sensory information and transmits it from the cerebral cortex to other areas of the brain and spinal cord.

**ventricles**—Hollow spaces within the brain that are filled with cerebrospinal fluid.

# Further Reading

## Books

Burnstein, John. *The Astounding Nervous System: How Does My Brain Work?* St. Catherines, Ontario: Crabtree Pub., 2009.

Parker, Steve. *Nervous System*. Mankato, Minn: New Forest Press/Black Rabbit Books, 2011.

Reilly, Kathleen M. *The Human Body*. White River Junction, Vt.: Nomad Press, 2008.

Stewart, Melissa. *You've Got Nerve!: The Secrets of the Brain and Nerves*. New York: Marshall Cavendish Benchmark, 2011.

## Internet Addresses

Discover Kids. *Your Gross & Cool Body*.
<http://yucky.discovery.com/flash/body>

Eric H. Chudler, Ph.D. (University of Washington)
*Neuroscience for Kids.*
<http://faculty.washington.edu/chudler/neurok.html>

# Index